Old ANTRIM

by
John Hanna

Even though the city of Dublin is some one hundred and twenty miles to the south of Antrim, there was a Dublin Road which headed out of Antrim in the general direction of the city. From this approach to the town it can be seen just how much the spire of All Saints' Parish Church, which was added to the building in 1816, dominated the skyline. The present Dublin Road forms part of a by-pass to the Lough Neagh side of the town, skirting the edge of the Sixmilewater River. This picture dates from 1952.

FURTHER READING

The books listed below were used by the author during his research. None of them are available from Stenlake Publishing. Those interested in finding out more are advised to contact their local bookshop or reference library.

Paul Holmes (illustrator) and Alastair Smyth, *Antrim, Town and Country*, Cottage Publications, 1999.
Alastair Smyth, *The Story of Antrim*, Nicholson and Bass, 1984.
Guy Warner and Jack Woods, *Belfast International Airport, Aviation at Aldergrove since 1918*, Colourpoint Books, 2001.
Grenfell Morton, *Railways in Ulster*, Friar's Bush Press, 1989.
Dr John A. Logan, *Massereene Golf Club*, Greystone Press, 1995.

ACKNOWLEDGEMENTS

The author would like to thank the following for their help: the Ulster Folk and Transport Museum, the Lough Neagh Discovery Centre at Oxford Island, Colette Lyness, Antrim Towns Development Co. Ltd, and Mr Delargy of Antrim.
    The publishers wish to thank both Robert Bonar, who contributed most of the pictures in this book, and Des Quail, who contributed the pictures on the front cover, pages 13 and 43 (lower), and the back cover.

The Lough Neagh Hotel was unique among Antrim's Hotels in that it had retail premises instead of a bar on the ground floor. J. Murphy, a jeweller, may have owned the shop on the right. He sold all sorts of souvenirs of Antrim in Irish marble and Irish bog oak. This photograph must have been taken close to Hallowe'en as the windows in the other shop are well stocked with Standard fireworks.

INTRODUCTION

That Antrim is 'old' is clear from its history. Early prehistoric people inhabited the region around Antrim and the area came under attack from a variety of peoples including the Celts in the fourth and fifth centuries. These were followed by Viking raiders who were attracted by the monastic houses which were established after St Patrick's ministry in the fifth century. In the Middle Ages it was the Anglo–Normans who invaded and settled, creating an 'Antrum' county. Donegore, and later Dunadry, became the administrative centre and also a place through which travellers passed on their way to the east and north of Ulster. The arrival of Scottish settlers in the seventeenth and eighteenth centuries led to the establishment of distinctive villages and towns.

The history of Antrim, like many other Irish towns, begins with the establishment of a monastery which was founded in AD 495, just thirty years after the death of St Patrick. This Aentrobh monastery was situated close to the present site of the Round Tower. 'Aentrobh' signifies 'the one ridge', as the town of Antrim was established on a ridge which ran from Tardree forest to Lough Neagh's Sandy Bay.

By 1596, where the Sixmilewater River could be forded at Masarine, the Elizabethan English had created their small settlement of Anthrona, which signifies 'a ford or ferry'. All Saints' Parish Church has a datestone of 1596 and written on it is 'Gall-Antrum', 'the Antrum of the English'. Later, Hugh Clotworthy, an army officer from Devon, supervised the construction of secure military quarters beside the old Norman motte which became the site of Antrim Castle. Clotworthy, who was knighted in 1617 and settled locally, was appointed High Sheriff of County Antrim and was granted Massereene.

In the early seventeenth century settlers from the lowlands of Scotland were encouraged to Antrim. They lived in clusters of thatched cottages which together became known as the 'Scotch Quarter' (later to become Church Street). Unfortunately, many of them could not find employment so to alleviate this problem Clotworthy persuaded Robert Wreyford from Devonshire to establish a cloth making industry, possibly at Riverside. The business expanded and the 'Refords' of Antrim became one of the first great Antrim linen families.

Clotworthy died in 1630 and was succeeded by his eldest son, Sir John, who was the first Lord Massereene and Baron of Lough Neagh. By 1641 rebellion was taking place in Ireland and the following year 4,000 Irish rebels led by Turlough O'Neill surrounded Antrim but were repelled. By 1648 Cromwellian soldiers were in the Antrim garrison and they came under attack by the Royalist army the following year. The Royalists failed to take the castle but razed the town to the ground. Later in the century the town also became the target for Jacobite armies and was not properly rebuilt for seventy years.

The next one hundred years was a period of continuous change, both among the churches and society. The ordinary people began to challenge the power of the aristocrats. In October 1791 the Society of United Irishmen was founded in Belfast. Their aim was the peaceful political reform of the Anglo–Irish Parliament in Dublin; instead another uprising occurred, beginning in Antrim in June 1798. This resulted in the Battle of Antrim which ended with much loss of life; however an amnesty for the rebels was agreed one month later. The Act of Union, which brought Irish government firmly under the control of the English, was passed in 1801.

By the mid-nineteenth century the social and economic conditions which had preserved the old traditions and cultural patterns of Antrim rural society were broken down by the coming of improved education, the railway and emigration. In 1865–66 the population was 2,138, with bleaching and malting being important industries along with the manufacture of linen, cotton and paper. It was the guaranteed supply of water which flowed through the valley of the Sixmilewater River which led to the development of the textile industry and created an influential middle-class which promoted Antrim's interests throughout the rest of the century.

By the 1900s mechanisation in farming along with the growth of the linen industry increased the prosperity of the region. The First World War saw both the estates of Shane's Castle and Antrim Castle accommodating thousands of troops, but also significant loss life amongst local soldiers. By the 1920s, however, this prosperity was not so marked and the town was said to be short of industry but long in dole queues. Rea's Saw Mills, the Antrim Linen Factory in Riverside, and York Street Flax Spinning in Muckamore were the main employers.

The Second World War saw many of the historic estates around Antrim once again become the training ground for Allied Forces and 20,000 USAAF forces were based there. The post-war period was one of little development and the town did not increase greatly in size – by 1961 the population was still only 3,000 people. However, the same features which had initially attracted the linen industry to the Antrim area led to the development of one of Northern Ireland's first man-made fibre plants when British Enkalon occupied a large site just outside the town in 1963. Within a year the company was employing 700 and was expanding rapidly.

In 1966 Antrim was designated a New Town. This led to an increase in population from around 7,500 to around 24,000 by 1977. With a slowdown in industrial growth in the area the population has since remained fairly static and is now around 25,500.

Market Square was the focal point of Antrim and this impressive building served a dual purpose. Built in 1726 for the grand sum of £150, the lower half was an arched market hall, while the courthouse occupied the upper floor. The small cupola on top was added in 1817. By 1836 the lower floor had been converted into a prison yard for prisoners attending trials and for confining drunkards and rioters. It was connected to the nearby police barracks by an underground tunnel to prevent prisoners escaping while on the short journey to the court. The building has been vacant since a new courthouse opened, although it has been purchased by Antrim Borough Council. Thompson's was a prominent shop dealing in fancy goods and was probably the distributor of a number of the postcards featured in this book. To the left of it was the Blue Bird Café and a public house was on the corner. An entry led to the Market Yard. This was where there were stalls for keeping animals, although the Castle Centre shopping centre now stands on this site.

The High Street was created by the Elizabethan English to link their castle and the parish church and as early as 1596 a typically English street with timbered buildings was developing. At one time the High Street was famous for its fourteen grocers' shops and twenty-two spirit dealers' premises. The Antrim Arms was the bar of Thompson's Hotel. It was still small in comparison with later years (the hotel was later renamed as the Antrim Arms Hotel). Here it is a simple two-storey building with an entrance to a yard at the rear. Two buildings along to the left was the post office.

FAIR DAY AT ANTRIM.

Fair Day was a very busy day in the daily life of Antrim folk. In 1665 the Massereenes had a patent to hold six fairs a year, but by the mid-nineteenth century only three remained. The Market Square and most of High Street were home to the annual livestock fair and in 1860 a weekly Thursday market was established for the buying and selling of local produce (a Thursday market is still held in the town). A hiring fair was also held in May and November. Fortunately many of the buildings in the centre of this picture are still standing. The building belonging to M. & A.H. Frew, who were the High Street's leading milliners, costumers and general drapers, is currently the Antrim Business Shop, incorporating the Tourist Information Office.

By the time of this picture the Antrim Arms had expanded to the right and the entrance to the yard had disappeared. It had become a three-storey building with bay windows. A.E. Barr's newsagent is next door and an early petrol pump can be seen next to the road. Ms Barr's brothers were cycle dealers and later ran a garage next door. Joe Barr later became a town commissioner. The castellated wall of the Castle may be seen at the north end of Market Square.

FAWCETT'S ANTRIM ARMS HOTEL, ANTRIM
HEADQUARTERS OF FAWCETT'S HOLIDAY TOURS, PARTY OF
TOURISTS LEAVING HOTEL FOR DAILY TOUR.

The Antrim Arms Hotel was one of five hotels on High Street. In 1902 it boasted the largest dining room in the town which could seat one hundred! When taken over by Sam Fawcett it became the Antrim Arms Hotel and a period of expansion took place. At the time of this picture in the 1920s the Antrim Arms had expanded further, taking in the complete building to the left of it, and building it up to the three-storey level. The hotel was destroyed by fire in the Spring of 1938 and never rebuilt due to the outbreak of the Second World War. Fawcett organised tours in open-air charabancs to the beautiful Antrim Coast, including the Giant's Causeway. Most of the tourists were mill workers from Lancashire. In 1929 it was reported that 6,000 tourists had been catered for. The small building next to the hotel was once a chemist's shop owned by F.T. Smith and is one of the few buildings remaining at this end of the street after the fire.

Today it is hard to imagine five hotels set next to one another on Antrim's Main Street. Three of them were actually side by side. The Massereene Arms Hotel boasted that it had a 'First Class Posting Establishment' attached to it and that the arrival and departure of all trains was attended. Eight post horses were attached to it. The other two hotels were Hall's, owned by Robert J. Hall, and the Adair Temperance Hotel, owned by Henry Adair. The front of Hall's Hotel, in between the other two, now has just a single entrance. The horse and cart are passing the entrance to Bridge Street. On this corner was Barney McQuillan's cobbler's shop.

The Massereene Arms Hotel was established in 1754, and was the headquarters of the military officers in the town during June of 1798 when the United Irishmen of Henry Joy McCracken marched on the town. At that time Antrim was the most important military base between Belfast and Londonderry. McCracken's men lost the Battle of Antrim and the rebellion was broken after other defeats at Saintfield and Ballynahinch. McCracken was executed in Belfast in July that year. The Massereene Arms, which no longer stands, extended to the rear over the river. Next door to it was the general store of Peter Conway. Chiefly he sold clothing, but also stocked anything he thought there was a ready market for. He remained open until 11 p.m. on Saturdays. The hotel site was redeveloped and is currently occupied by JJB Sports and Peacock's shop.

This view up the High Street shows the wide road that was built to link the Castle to the parish church and beyond. All the main streets were 'macadamised' in the 1930s. Gas lamps had lit the streets from 1855 and the electric street lighting system was switched on in 1929.

By the time this photograph was taken in 1927 the number of telephones around the High Street had grown in number. The two-storey building, with the five windows on the upper floor, next to the Antrim Arms Hotel, had not yet been taken over as part of the hotel.

A wonderful picture of the different modes of transport around Antrim in the 1920s – a cart, a motorbike with a sidecar, and an open tourer. Hall's Family and Commercial Hotel was established in 1897. In the early days of motoring it was important for hotels to be recognised by the various motoring organisations whose badges were proudly displayed on the front of the hotels. This picture was taken before the hotel's façade was altered. At this time there were two entrances, one for the hotel and the other for the bar.

The broad sweep of Antrim's Main Street pictured from the tower of All Saints' Parish Church. The increasing prosperity of the town by the early 1950s is obvious from the well-kept road verges and the cherry trees (gifted to the town by Henry Dupré Malkin Barton) which were planted alongside the road and the public telephone box. Nicholl continues to operate several shops on the street and most of the buildings in the picture remain intact. The tall building set away from Church Street is the Methodist Chapel which was built in 1805. It is now a branch library.

CHURCH STREET, ANTRIM.

The area of Church Street was formerly known as the Scotch Quarter because from the 1590s Scots people settled in this part of town, erecting clusters of thatched cottages. The picture, which appeared on a postcard posted in 1915, looks south towards Townhead. The shop on the left was Miss Jameson's, a grocery which also sold china goods.

Church Street, Antrim.

In the 1930s Church Street was the centre for outfitters' shops, among them William Dougall's, John Lawlor's and Wright's. Mrs Nicholl's confectionery shop was established in 1924. This card, posted in 1915, shows that a number of thatched dwellings still existed at that time. The trees on the right mark the entrance to the Methodist Chapel, while the thatched cottages were taken away to provide space for the A6 by-pass.

Castle Street, Antrim.

Castle Street ran from the Market Square out of town to the north and east. The Castle grounds are on the left along with the 'Frenchman's House' and the Royal Irish Constabulary barracks. Samuel Rea's Antrim Saw Mills operated in Castle Street and there were also the premises of a spirit dealer called Patrick Magill. Another shop was McKeown's. Unfortunately all the buildings on this street were later demolished. However, one of the Castle Street's shops, Rea's, and the barracks were removed and rebuilt stone by stone at the Ulster Folk and Transport Museum at Cultra.

FOUNTAIN STREET, ANTRIM.

6685

Formerly known as Townhead, Fountain Street derived its new name from the fact that it was the site of one of the town's water pumps. This card illustrates the view that all travellers would have had as they approached Antrim from Belfast, before the building of the motorway and by-pass. Miss A. Mackey sold confectionery and light groceries from her shop in Fountain Street, which was also well-known for such grocers as William French, Robert McCrory, and Thomas Swann. The houses on the right all still exist, but the houses beside Hargrove's petrol pumps made way for the entrance to the North East Institute for Further and Higher Education.

18

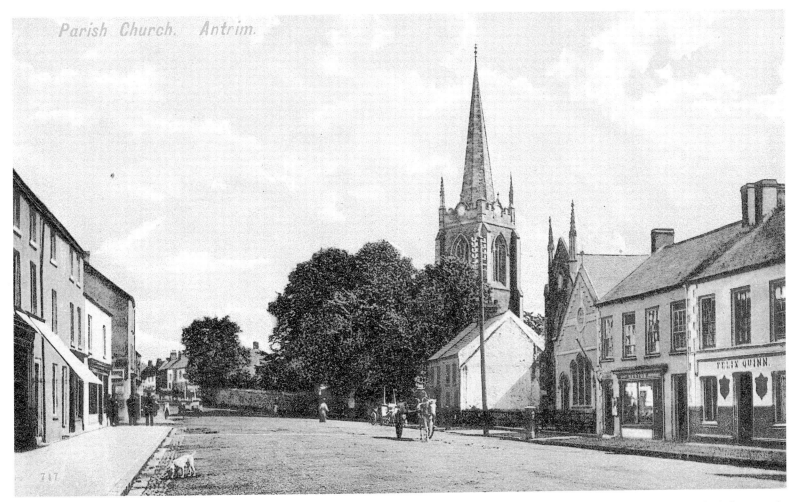

The original datestone of All Saints' Parish Church is 1596, which indicates that it was the fourth Anglican church to be built in Ireland. Unfortunately the Scottish Covenanting army of Major General Robert Munro burned the church to the ground in 1649. The thatched roof of its replacement (today's church) was also burnt during the 1798 rebellion. The Rev. George Macartney, Episcopalian vicar of Antrim and Templepatrick, was responsible for the addition of the church's tower in 1812, followed by the lofty spire which was added four years later. The houses between it and the High Street Presbyterian Church were knocked down to make a wider entrance to Riverside. The public house of Felix Quinn is now the Steeple Inn.

The High Street Presbyterian Church was originally called the Second Antrim Presbyterian Church and was built in 1837 at a total cost of around £940. The building of a new larger church meant that it was no longer required for religious purposes. Renamed Church House, it now houses offices. Orr School was built in 1900 and was named after Rev. John Orr who was the first minister of the High Street congregation. Its hall could be divided in two by sliding partitions and it had a fine heating system for the winter. The building is now an electric appliance showroom.

This postcard was posted in 1908 and shows All Saints' Parish Church viewed from Riverside (Mill Row). Set into the wall on the right is the church datestone of 1596. Workers from the nearby linen mills occupied the thatched houses on this street. The celebrated Puritan English vicar, John Ridge, was, as early as 1619, the first recorded preacher in the church. It was thought that a medieval church existed on this site as early as 1306. It has strong links with the Massereene Family, some of whom are buried in the vaults beneath the church. The parents of the writer, Dr Alexander Irvine, are buried in the small graveyard seen behind the church. In 1946 his ashes were brought back from the United States, where he had been minister of a church on New York's Fifth Avenue, and buried beside his parents.

This view of the south bank of the Sixmilewater River from 1928 shows the contrast of the more modern terrace houses in Riverside with the earlier thatched cottages closer to Church Street. The houses on the right of Riverside have little changed today.

ST. CONGALL R.C. CHURCH, ANTRIM.

Before 1818 there was no Catholic church in Antrim and Mass was celebrated at a number of outdoor locations. However, that year £1,400 was subscribed to enable Father Bernard McAuley to erect the town's first chapel. That was replaced in 1870 by this building, St Comgall's, at the junction of Castle Street and Oriel Street. The church at one time had its walls painted black with contrasting cement and with its Italian-style tower remains a distinctive landmark in the town.

First Antrim Presbyterian Church.

In 1731 a group of Presbyterians erected a Meeting House in Mill Row (Riverside). By 1834 the congregation had outgrown this building and a new church was built with access to Church Street. Unfortunately this was burnt down in 1860. It was rebuilt, and the interior was altered in 1903. From the outside the building has retained its appearance from the 1800s. At its front are two sturdy Doric columns, and a façade in the Greek-revival style. The columns are copies of the ancient portico at Thorieus in Greece, but are in contrast to the interior of the church, which is characteristically plain. To the left is the Bruce Memorial School which had around a hundred pupils. Behind it is the sexton's house. A large church hall replaced these buildings in 1994.

Massereene Bridge was built in 1708 by Lord Massereene and John O'Neill Esq. as a gift to the people of Antrim. A Mr George Jackson and Mr Alexander Cornwell were the overseers of the construction. The bridge was repaired and widened in 1857, the contractor being William Vance, who was Chairman of the Town Commissioners and owned a hardware store in High Street. The modernisation of Antrim is evident from this picture from 1952.

Riverside, Antrim.

G.W. Thompson
Antrim.

Formerly known as Mill Row, Riverside was the industrial district of Antrim during the eighteenth and nineteenth centuries. The Sixmilewater River provided the focus for this and a paper mill was established as early as 1776, joined by a brewery in 1807 and a corn mill later in the 1800s. The brewery was built on the original site of the House of Correction and the stocks. In 1850 Riverside became the centre for linen manufacture when Boals of Ballymena built a linen mill on the site of the paper mill. Boals was taken over by Lamonts, also of Ballymena, who continued to operate it until the late twentieth century. Unfortunately the mills are now gone, but the view from this spot today is very similar.

26

POGUE'S ENTRY, ANTRIM.

Pogue's Entry was one of a number of 'entries' leading off the length of Church Street where the labouring classes lived. The houses were generally smoky and damp one-storey thatched cottages. Pogue's Entry was made famous by the fact that it was the setting for the best-selling book *My Lady of the Chimney Corner* by Dr Alexander Irvine. In 1931 he wrote that 'poverty inadequately describes the condition of life in that entry', an opinion borne out by the conditions of surroundings and the dress of the children in the picture. The mud-floored stone cottage of Alexander Irvine, on the left of the entry, is preserved in its original state. The doorway in the centre leads out to Church Street and is still the entrance to the cobbled yard today.

Railway Station — Antrim

While the Railway Age began in Ulster in 1839, it was not until 1848 that the Belfast & Ballymena Railway Company reached Antrim. Delays were caused by uncertainty about how the route should run up to the Antrim Plateau. The arrival of the railway in Antrim encouraged tourism and the growth of Antrim's hotels. It also enabled the importation and exportation of farm produce and encouraged the expansion of the linen industry. However, the coming of the railway also undermined some local industries, such as Antrim Brewery, by bringing in better and cheaper products. At the time of this postcard the Midland Railway was operating the line; 2001 saw the reintroduction of the direct Belfast to Antrim line.

"DUNLUCE CASTLE" AT ANTRIM

Engine no. 74, 'Dunluce Castle', was one of seven Class U2 locomotives built in 1924 by the North British Locomotive Company of Glasgow. Another eleven were built at York Road, Belfast. It was at first based at Coleraine and Ballymena, but during the Second World War it was based at Whitehead, before moving to York Road in the 1950s. The engine was withdrawn in 1963, having completed 1,135,484 miles in service. It is now beautifully restored and on permanent display at the magnificent Railway Galleries of the Ulster Folk and Transport Museum.

Deerpark Bridge is a picturesque feature of the Antrim Castle gardens. Constructed in the mid-eighteenth century, it is built from basalt rubble and has six semicircular arches. It would have originally provided access to a public road leading to Lough Neagh and the rest of the Massereene estate, the Deerpark.

Known as the Barbican Gate this was originally the main entrance to the Castle. Possibly designed by John Bowden, it was built about 1818 with neo-Tudor towers. The gatekeeper would have lived behind the windows over the gate. The arms of the Massereene and Ferrard families are displayed on the archway above the gate. The family motto reads *Per Angusta ad Augusta* – 'Through hard times to prosperity'.

Antrim Castle was built in various stages between 1610 and 1666 and was originally built in a half 'H' plan, comprising a main east-facing block and two long wings. During 1812/13 it was remodelled in mock-Gothic style and additional renovations were carried out during the Victorian era. The Massereene and Ferrard families occupied the Castle between 1610 and 1922. The octagonal tower, part of an extension on the south face which was added in 1887, is now all that remains.

During a grand ball on the night of 28 October 1922 the Castle caught fire and was destroyed. It remained a ruin until 1970 when it was completely demolished. At the time it was assumed that the fire was started maliciously, but a subsequent claim for compensation was turned down on the basis that the fire could have been accidental. This is the front of the building with its square cornered towers. Above the main entrance may be seen the sculptured panels and tablets incorporating inscriptions and coats-of-arms.

29/50. ANTRIM FROM CASTLE GARDENS.

The gardens, situated adjacent to the Courthouse, were created by Lord Massereene between 1680 and 1715. Europe's leading landscape designer of the seventeenth century, Andre Le Notre, was engaged in the original design to create echoes of his masterpiece at the Palace at Versailles which he designed for Louis XIV. Margaretta, Lady Massereene, incorporated the round pond and the hedge-bordered canal in 1820. The design for these was by William Vitrius Morrison. The formal patterned garden also had a productive purpose, supplying the Castle with herbs for cooking and medicinal purposes. The parterre had disappeared by 1857. In the 1990s the gardens, including the parterre were re-created and opened to the public.

Massereene, Antrim.

The name Massereene is derived from 'Masaregna'. The Barony of Antrum was renamed Masaregna (which translates as 'the Queen's Hill') by the northern O'Neills around 1400, in memory of one of their clan queens who drowned in the Sixmilewater River. In 1838 the Ordnance Survey memoir stated that Massereene was a fisherfolk's shanty hamlet where 'they pay little or no rent, own no land or boast not more than a little garden; break down fences in the neighbourhood for fuel, trespass on plantations for the same purpose, steal poultry and commit various depradations'. It is said that when Lord Massereene visited his smithy one day he found him working outside in the most inclement weather beside the thatched houses and decided there and then to build the smith a proper forge. As seen in the picture on the approach to Massereene Bridge the road rises and the lower windows and doors on the white houses are partially below the level of the road. The building on the right is now a carpet shop.

Lord Massereene built the forge in 1887. With its horseshoe doorway, there is no doubt about the building's original function. In the winter the forge was often a place of refuge, and before the advent of television it was the hub of attraction for many of the boys brought up in the area. It has been Antrim's most photographed building, and is currently a paint and wallpaper shop.

Greenmount House and its two hundred-acre estate belonged to the Thompson family. Robert Thompson rebuilt the grand manor house at Greenmount in 1820. In the eighteenth century the family owned bleach mills on the estate, and other businesses in Ireland as well as some as far afield as the West Indies. This made the family powerful enough in the area to challenge the political power of the aristocratic Massereene family by standing for election. The estate was purchased by the Department of Agriculture in 1910, and opened in 1912 as an agricultural college with eleven students. This picture dates from 1952; students still study agriculture and horticulture there today.

The shores of Lough Neagh were ideally suited to the creation of a golf links and Lord Massereene, the 11th Viscount Massereene and Ferrard, granted the land for this purpose in 1895. He became the president of the club which became known as Massereene Golf Club. Both the 12th and 13th viscounts were also presidents. For a short period after it opened it was an eighteen-hole course, although two years later it was reduced to nine holes. It was 1964 before the course returned to an eighteen-hole layout. This postcard was posted in 1912 and shows clearly the type of dress, including wide-brimmed hats, which lady golfers of the time wore.

The clubhouse was built in 1901 and the club has sought to preserve it over the years. In the beginning it served as little more than a shelter, but in 1927 a range was provided so that tea could be made on competition days. Three years later water was piped to it, enabling wash basins to be installed, and a dressing room for ladies was provided. It is still part of the buildings of Massereene Golf Club today.

On the day of the coronation of King George V, 22 June 1911, Antrim had all its public buildings and many dwelling houses decorated in a manner which showed much taste. Eight decorative arches spanned the streets. Massereene Brass and Reed Band marched from the Massereene School to Townhead and after returning to the Courthouse steps, where the National Anthem was sung (pictured), the town's school pupils marched to the Agricultural Showgrounds. Later in the evening the band rendered some fine musical selections, which were much enjoyed by the crowd assembled in Market Square.

The Cutts, or Corrigan's Cutts, is where the Sixmilewater River enters Lough Neagh and is an ideal place for boating activities. The Corrigans were a family who lived on the Randalstown Road. This picture dates from 1911. Today it is the site of Antrim Marina which has a capacity for fifty boats. Close to this spot Kay Don practised in his *Miss England 2* for an attempt on the waterspeed record in 1931.

Lough Neagh is the largest freshwater lake in the British Isles, covering 383 square kilometres. These boats may well be the pleasure cruisers *White Heather* and *Peacehaven*. In the past the lough has been the scene of many naval battles such as the bloody Anglo–Irish battle of 1643 and the Vikings at one time controlled these waters. In Elizabethan times armies from a garrison at Carrickfergus were able to travel west by going down the Sixmilewater River and across Lough Neagh. Until recently *The Maid of Antrim* ran cruises on the lough, but she was sold in 2000.

The steam-driven *Lough Neagh Queen* operated in the early part of the twentieth century and pioneered the development of the Lough Neagh Cruising Company. This company ran the *White Heather* and the *Peacehaven* which was registered in 1927. Each vessel took thirty tourists on excursion cruises on the lough. Between 1820 and 1860 merchant steamboats operated on the lough and it was possible to sail from Belfast through canals to the lough and then along the Lower Bann to the North Atlantic.

Harry Ferguson, one of Northern Ireland's famous inventors and an aviation pioneer, first took flight at Aldergrove Aerodrome in 1910. His plane was a thirty-five horsepower eight cylinder monoplane. Aldergrove was also a training station for the Royal Flying Corps in 1917, before becoming an important RAF aerodrome.

Side View of Hangers, Aldergrove.

In September 1963 the Northern Ireland's civilian airport at Nutt's Corner was transferred to Aldergrove. The first civilian flights took place from Aldergrove in May 1933 when the return fare to Scotland was £5. While still retaining its military connections, it continued to expand and became Belfast International Airport in 1983. This card was posted in 1939 and the aircraft are RAF biplanes.

Nutt's Corner was developed as an airbase as a consequence of the wartime airfield construction programme. The plan included relatively long runways and concrete parking aprons. In December 1946 it replaced Belfast Harbour as Northern Ireland's civil airport. International traffic from Nutt's Corner, which began in the late 1950s, was all charter work. The aircraft pictured were operated by British European Airways, later to become British Airways. This picture dates from around 1952.

Moyelena Bridge and Weir, Muckamore, Antrim.

This is a fast flowing section of the Sixmilewater River, where it flows through the high banks of the Vale of Moylena. It is now a very wooded area, just below the road at Muckamore. Little remains of the house on the right, but the bridge still crosses the river between the two posts. Across the road is a small cemetery and the obelisk which can be seen amongst the trees marks the burial ground of one Josias Cunningham of Glencairn, Belfast, who died in 1870. His family members continue to be buried there.

Moylena Banks, Antrim.

In 1919 when this card was posted, this house stood just a few hundred yards down river from the weir. A mill-race is led off at a point beside the weir, running parallel to the river, but at a higher level. Close to this point there are the remains of a water wheel, which provided the power for a 'beetling engine' which was used in finishing linen cloth. The noise from these engines could be heard all along the Moylena Banks. This house was owned by the York Street Flax Spinning Company and in the 1950s it housed four Antrim families – the McCombs, the Tuffs, the Campbells and the Steeles – some members of which worked for the company.

This was one of a number of bridges built so that the railway could reach the town. The bridge has a datestone of 1847 which was a year before the arrival of the first train in Antrim. Little has changed in this view save for the road being widened. High vehicles obviously have some difficulty finding the centre of the arch as much damage can now be seen beneath the bridge. The men are sitting on an older bridge over the Sixmilewater River close to Muckamore.

Muckamore, Antrim.

The name Muckamore may have arisen from the fact that the earth in the area was found to be so fertile that the ancient Irish christened the land where the Sixmilewater enters Lough Neagh *Magh-Comair* – the plain of the confluence. Muckamore Abbey was founded in AD 585 by Colmanellus at the upper entrance to the Vale of Moylinne. The York Street Flax Spinning Company had a large mill here and these are mill workers' terraced homes. The larger houses at each end of the road housed the 'gaffers'. The house on the left of the terrace was the post office and the one at the other end was the general store. These houses remain, as do another row behind them called 'Raceview' which were closer to the mill race.